Drew Brees

The Inspirational Story of Football Superstar Drew Brees

D1509752

presentation of the information is without contract or any type of guarantee assurance.

The trademarks that are used are without any consent, and the publication of the trademark is without permission or backing by the trademark owner. All trademarks and brands within this book are for clarifying purposes only and are the owned by the owners themselves, not affiliated with this document.

Table Of Contents

Introduction

As the title already implies, this is a book about [The Inspirational Story of Football Superstar Drew Brees] and how he rose from his life in Austin, Texas to becoming one of today's leading and most-respected football players. In his rise to superstardom, Drew has inspired not only the youth, but fans of all ages throughout the world.

This book also portrays the struggles that Drew has had to overcome during his early childhood years, his teen years, and up until he became what he is today. A notable source of inspiration is Drew's own foundation that was named after him, as well as his consistent support of other charitable organizations. He continues to serve as the humble, mild-mannered superstar in a sport that glorifies flashy plays and mega personalities.

Combining incredible accuracy, an elite football IQ, quick feet, and superior coordination, Drew has shown the ability to impact a game in a variety of ways. From being a young athlete who could play multiple sports to becoming one of the greatest quarterbacks of his generation, you'll learn here how this man has risen to the ranks of the best football players today.

Thanks again for downloading this book. I hope you are able to take some lessons from Drew's life and apply them to your own!

Chapter 1:

Youth & Family Life

Drew Christopher Brees was welcomed to the world on January 15th, 1979. His father, Eugene Wilson Brees II, was a trial lawyer and nicknamed "Chip". His mother, Mina Ruth, was an attorney. The family lived in Austin, Texas during Drew's youth and it has since been revealed that Drew was named after former Dallas Cowboys star wide receiver, Drew Pearson.

Drew was the first-born child of his family, two and a half years older than his brother Reid. When Drew was seven years of age, his parents decided to divorce, but shared custody of their two boys. Drew and Reid would split time between the homes of both their mother and father, enjoying the presence of both parents throughout their youth. Furthermore, Drew also gained a younger half-sister, Audrey, from his father's second marriage.

Drew was born into an athletic family, as his father had played basketball for Texas A&M University's men's basketball team while his mother was a former all-state high school athlete in three different sports. Additionally, his uncle from his mother's side, Marty Atkins, was the starting quarterback for the University of Texas Longhorns college football team. Marty earned All-American honors during his time as a Longhorn. Drew's grandfather was also the third-winningest high school football coach in the state of Texas during his three decade tenure.

By the time he was in middle school, Drew was playing flag football consistently. He showed early interest in the sport and developed the work ethic to hone his skill-set as a youngster. Drew chose to attend Westlake High School upon entering the ninth grade and had developed a passion for multiple sports by this time. He lettered in baseball, basketball, and football during his time at Westlake.

He was so good at baseball that he considered the possibility of playing college baseball after his graduation from high school. However, after he overcame a torn ACL in his junior year, Drew returned to perform at an elite level in his senior season. He was able to lead Westlake High School to a 16-0 record while also bringing the state championship back home. Personally, he was awarded the Texas 5A Most Valuable Offensive Player Award for his outstanding, consistent play throughout the season.

His statistics for his entire high school varsity career included a 64% completion percentage for over 5,000 yards, to go along with 50 touchdowns. In his senior season alone, Drew threw for over 3,500 yards and 31 touchdowns. As the starting quarterback for the team, Drew's record was a combined 28-0-1.

Drew gained much attention from scouts and experts from the collegiate ranks and went on to be named to the Texas All-State football team, as well as the honorable mention for USA Today's All-USA high school football team. Despite all of these accolades, Drew was not considered an elite prospect for the collegiate level, mainly because of his lack of height - which was perceived to be a limiting factor in his potential.

Drew's dream to play for the Texas Longhorns or Texas A&M Aggies did not come to fruition, as the schools did not actively recruit him. However, he did receive offers to play for Purdue University and the University of Kentucky. After evaluating his options, Drew decided that Purdue's academic prestige would provide him a better overall experience as a student-athlete.

Chapter 2:

College

Drew started his college career off without any immediate expectations. He did not start a game during his first season with the team. However, he was able to use the time to learn the offensive playbook and build his body up. After using this time to prepare himself for a bigger role in the upcoming season, Drew was ready to experience the starting role.

As he entered his sophomore season at Purdue, Drew was named the starting quarterback by Coach Joe Tiller. The team ran a spread offense that put pressure on the defensive backs and linebackers to cover an unusually wide distance. While spread offenses are the norm in college football now, at the time this offense was rather unorthodox and many teams did not have effective strategies to combat this philosophy.

Drew posted solid statistics in his sophomore season at Purdue and earned the team's trust by season's end. Although he threw 20 interceptions, he was able to complete 39 touchdown passes and total almost 4,000 yards passing. This impressive show of dominance on the field, as well as his ability to lead his teammates in the locker room and in the huddle, led Drew to being named the offensive captain of the team during his junior and senior seasons.

After another impressive year as a junior, Drew faced the dilemma of whether to declare for the 2000 NFL Draft or to return for his senior year at Purdue. After some thought, he would eventually decide to return for his senior season. Not only was he able to earn his degree in industrial management but he led the Boilermakers to a win over top-ranked Ohio State University in one of the most memorable games in Purdue football history. The team was also able to defeat the Michigan Wolverines in their journey to winning the Big Ten Championship - their first in over three decades.

The team would finish the regular season with an invitation to the 2001 Rose Bowl. Purdue faced the Washington Huskies in the Rose Bowl and would suffer a ten point loss, but it was a successful season for the program nonetheless. On a personal note, Drew had garnered much national attention for his gritty performances and ability to keep cool under pressure - a trait that intrigued professional scouts.

He would go on to become a finalist for the Davey O'Brien Award, an award that is given to the nation's best quarterback every year. He also won the Maxwell Award as a senior and finished in the top four in the Heisman Trophy voting during his last two seasons. Drew was also taking care of business in the classroom, as he earned Academic All-American honors in his senior season. He also earned Academic All-Big Ten honors in three different years while he was at Purdue. Lastly, he was given the Leonard Wilson Award for his dedication and unselfishness.

By the time Drew graduated from the school in 2001, he had set Big Ten records in total career passing yards, total touchdown passes, total offensive yards, and completions. At the time, he also held the NCAA record for most pass attempts in a game (83) and the longest pass ever (99 yards).

Drew achieved massive success at the college level just as he did in the high school ranks, however his lack of height would limit him once again as the 2001 NFL Draft neared. Despite having the tools necessary to be a starting quarterback in the National Football League, many scouts predicted him to fall out of the first round because they believed his height would limit his abilities at the next level. Furthermore, some around the league concluded that Drew did not have the arm strength necessary to beat NFL defensive backs over the top and that he was mainly a product of the spread offense system. Once again, Drew would have to prove his doubters wrong.

Chapter 3:

Professional Life

Drew slipped past the first round and into the second round, but not by much. He was chosen by the San Diego Chargers with the first pick in the second round and was the second quarterback taken overall - after Michael Vick of Virginia Tech. Drew would join fellow rookie LaDainian Tomlinson on a team that was one of the worst in the league the year before. Drew would choose the number nine in tribute to one of his childhood idols, baseball great, Ted Williams.

Drew's first year was spent mainly on the bench, as he only appeared in one regular season game. He spent the season learning the offense and preparing for his opportunity. Drew's opportunity finally came in training camp of his second season. After a strong showing, Drew would be given the starting job over veteran Doug Flutie for the first game of the regular season. He went on to start all sixteen regular season games for the Chargers and showed a strong grasp of the offense, completing almost 61% of his passes. The team finished with a .500 record of 8-8 and did not make the postseason. However, Drew did show some potential for the future.

Drew's third season was a struggle. He got off to a rocky start and was replaced by Doug Flutie after a few games into the season. He would finish the season with only 15 touchdowns to go with 11 interceptions. The team did not fare well for the season and Drew headed into the off-season unsure about his future. However, Drew knew that the only thing he could control was his work ethic and preparation. He spent the off-season learning as much as he could and developed his game to a level that it had never been at before.

After the San Diego Chargers drafted Phillip Rivers in the 2004 NFL Draft, there was word that the Chargers' starting job was up for grabs. Nonetheless, Drew was named the starter for the 2004 season and his preparation paid off. He started a total of fifteen games for the season and was able to lead the team to a 12-4 regular season record. Most importantly, the Chargers were able to win the AFC West and earn a playoff berth.

Personally, the season served as a breakout year for Drew - as he would post career highs in all of the key statistical categories. His 65% completion percentage along with 27 touchdowns and only 7 interceptions, combined with a total of over 3,000 passing yards, earned him an invitation to the 2004 Pro Bowl. Additionally, Drew was named the NFL Comeback Player of the Year for the 2004-05 season.

Drew became a free agent after the 2004-05 season and he was unsure about his future. The team had already committed a great deal of money to Phillip Rivers and did not publicly announce either as their quarterback for the future. Nevertheless, Drew signed a "franchise player" contract with the Chargers and continued to start for the 2005-06 season.

The 2005 season would be another career year for Drew, as he posted career highs in all key statistical categories once again. He threw for over 3,500 yards and had the 10th best passer rating in the entire league. Unfortunately, Drew tore the labrum in his right shoulder (his throwing shoulder) during a freak accident in the last game of the regular season. It was concluded by team doctors and coaches that Drew would need to undergo arthroscopic surgery to repair the damage. Nevertheless, he was still selected as the first alternate to the 2005 Pro Bowl for the AFC team. However, because of the injury he was scratched from the game in favor of Jake Plummer.

Drew was offered a back-heavy, performance based salary by the Chargers after the season, approximately a $50 million contract that spanned five years. However, the deal would only pay him $2 million in base salary for his first year under contract and it was not ideal for his production value to the team. This showed a lack of confidence by the Chargers organization and Drew, along with his agent, decided that he was worth more than what was being offered.

The New Orleans Saints showed great interest in Drew and he met with the team during the offseason. The team was very interested in his star potential and believed that the situation could be mutually beneficial for both parties.

Drew eventually agreed to a deal that paid $10 million in guaranteed money for his first season with the team. Furthermore, he would be paid an additional $12 million in his second year, along with an option to leave. By March, both parties agreed to a six year deal that would pay out $60 million in total.

The team was coming off a horrendous 2005 season in which they were forced to bounce around during the season because of the damage incurred by Hurricane Katrina. They essentially did not play a single home game for the entire year and finished with a 3-13 record for the season. First year coach Sean Payton and first year quarterback Drew Brees represented a fresh start for the franchise and brought hope, if not at least a distraction from their misery, to the people of New Orleans. The team would finish the season with a 10-6 regular season record and were able to win the NFC South division title.

Drew took his game to the next level once again, as he tossed for almost 4,500 yards and finished third in the National Football League in total touchdown passes. He made the Pro Bowl once again, this time for the NFC, and was showing that he could possibly become one of the elite quarterbacks in the game. The season also catapulted him into the conversation for the

MVP award, as he finished second to former teammate and longtime friend, LaDainian Tomlinson.

In the postseason, the Saints went on to win a tough game against the Philadelphia Eagles by the score of 27-24. The game was monumental for the city of New Orleans because it was played in the Louisiana Superdome and was the first postseason game since Hurricane Katrina. The team's next game was against the Chicago Bears in the NFC Championship Game. Unfortunately, the Bears handled the Saints fairly easily, beating them with a score of 39-14. Despite a disappointing end to the season, the franchise was clearly heading in the right direction and the fans were in great support of Drew and new coach, Sean Payton.

Drew would continue his excellent play in the 2007 regular season, as the offense was clicking and he threw for almost 4,500 yards for the second consecutive year. He was also able to tie a team record of 28 touchdowns in a season. Sean Payton's offensive system allowed Drew to thrive, as he would go on to break Rich Gannon's NFL record of completions in a single season - finishing the year with 440. Unfortunately, the team's success did not correlate with Drew's individual statistics, as the team finished the year with a 7-9 record and missed the NFC Playoffs.

Drew's 2008 season served as another stepping stone in his career. He solidified his place among the games best quarterbacks when he posted a season of over 5,000 yards through the air. He was only 15 yards short of the NFL record for the most passing yards in a single season, held by Dan Marino. He was also only the second quarterback in the history of the game to throw for over 5,000 yards in a season. Drew threw for over 300 yards in ten different games and it led to him being named the AP 2008 Offensive Player of the Year.

After two straight years of missing the postseason, the New Orleans Saints entered the 2009 regular season with a renewed focus. Drew set a career high with six touchdown passes in his first game of the season when the team played the Detroit Lions. He threw for 358 yards in the effort and the team looked sharp in all three facets of the game. The following week was no different, as the Saints beat the Philadelphia Eagles around in a 48-22 win. After the first two games of the season, Drew had already totaled nine touchdown passes.

The team would go through their struggles as the season went on but were able to continue winning games in whatever fashion they could. There were a few come-from-behind desperation victories along with some blowouts, but the team stood at 8-0 at the midway point in the season. It was their best start in franchise history and many experts around the league were claiming that the Saints looked like the favorites to come out of the NFC.

In Week 12, Drew performed about as well as a professional quarterback can, when he led the Saints to a 38-17 victory against the New England Patriots on *Monday Night Football*. Statistically, Drew totaled over 370 yards passing and threw for five touchdowns. Also, his passer rating for the game was a perfect 158.3. The team would also march to victory in its next two games as well and reach a point where their record was a perfect 13-0. The team looked extremely sharp on offensive, defense, and special teams, while Coach Sean Payton had his players believing in their swagger.

Despite a loss to the Dallas Cowboys in their next game, the team was still confident in the direction that it was heading in. Coach Sean Payton decided to rest Drew the last game of the season to avoid any risk of injury because the team had already locked up the number one overall seed in the NFC Playoff race. As the Saints entered the Playoffs, expectations were high and Drew found himself in a position that he was not used to. He was finally considered the "favorite" instead of the underdog role that he thrived in. Nonetheless, Drew would show great leadership skills in getting his teammates prepared for the competition they would face.

In the divisional round, the Saints destroyed the Arizona Cardinals in a 45-14 rout, advancing them to the NFC Championship game. There, they would face a talented Minnesota Vikings team that would take them to overtime. The Saints were able to prevail in the nail-biter, winning by a score of 31-28. Finally, the Saints made it to the Super Bowl for the first time in team history.

In Super Bowl XLIV, the Saints faced off against the Indianapolis Colts and it was one of the most anticipated games in recent football history. Despite the fact that Hurricane Katrina had been a few years behind them, the Saints players showed pride in the city and made it known that they wanted to bring a title back to New Orleans. This was received very well by the national media and Saints fans began to appear all over the country. For the game, the Saints were able to defeat the Colts by a score of 31-17. Drew found himself in the record books once again when he completed a Super Bowl record of 32 passes. He was awarded the Super Bowl Most Valuable Player Award and Bourbon Street did not sleep for the next few weeks.

After the season ended, Drew was honored by many organizations, including Sports Illustrated, who named him their 2010 Sportsman of the Year - both for his Super Bowl victory and the charitable work that he had done. He was also named the Male Athlete of the Year by the Associated Press. He made the Pro-Bowl, was runner up in the AP Most Valuable Player award, named the Offensive Player of the Year, and finished the season with a completion percentage of over %70 - a new NFL record. Not bad.

The Saints were able to avoid the infamous Super Bowl hangover in 2010. The team had a strong season once again, finishing with an 11-5 record. However, they were eliminated in the Wild Card round of the NFC Playoffs by the Seattle Seahawks. Drew was named to another Pro Bowl and was ranked as the ninth best player in the entire NFL. The ranking was done by his peers.

Drew would go on to have one of the greatest statistical seasons in the history of the NFL during his 2011 regular season. He finished the year in the league lead for completion percentage, touchdown passes, and passing yards - considered the "Triple Crown" for quarterbacks. His 46 touchdown passes were a franchise record and his total of 5,476 passing yards was an NFL record. He averaged an NFL record of 342.25 yards per game and had passed the 4,000 yard mark in only the twelfth game of the season.

Drew became the first quarterback in the history of the league to throw for more than 4,000 yards and complete more than 30 touchdown passes in four consecutive years. In total, Drew was able to set six different regular season records during the 2011-12 season and his year would go down as one the greatest statistical shows by any quarterback ever. The Saints would go on to beat the Detroit Lions in the NFC Wild Card game but would lose in the Divisional Round to the San Francisco 49ers.

After the season, Drew found himself in an unfamiliar contractual position from any other point in his career. He finally had the leverage to command a big time contract and the Saints delivered on their end. By mid-July, the two sides agreed to a $100 million contract that spanned five years. Furthermore, the contract guaranteed $60 million - the largest ever guaranteed money for an NFL contract. Unlike the back-heavy deal that Drew was offered with the Chargers, the Saints gave him the first $40 million in the first year of his deal - a sign that he was well-trusted and that the team had full confidence in him going forward.

By Week 5 of the 2012 season, Drew found himself in the record books once again when he had his 48th consecutive game with a touchdown pass. Despite all of the troubles surrounding the team from the "Bountygate" scandal, the team was able to hold it together thanks to the leadership of Drew and other veterans on the team. The team's defense would take a hit without many of their key players and coaches, but the offense was able to sustain itself throughout most of the year. The team finished under .500 at a 7-9 record, and missed the NFC Playoffs. Drew went on to make the 2013 Pro Bowl as an injury replacement for Robert Griffin III.

Drew hit some impressive career milestones in his 2013 campaign. In Week 12, he was able to move into 5th on the all-time list for total passing yards, passing legend Warren Moon in the process. In Week 14, Drew became the fastest player to reach 50,000 career passing yards, as well as only the fifth player to ever accomplish the feat. The team would finish the year with an 11-5 record and would beat the Philadelphia Eagles in the Wild Card round of the Playoffs. Once again, the Saints would not be able to get past the Divisional Round, as they lost to the future Super Bowl winner, Seattle Seahawks.

Chapter 4:

Personal Adult Life

Drew is certainly one of the most unique superstars in the NFL and is not afraid to show his passion in the interests he holds both on and off the field. He has publicly stated that he is a Christian and became seriously committed to his faith at the age of seventeen. His faith in God is strong and he keeps a deep connection to the church and allows God to handle the difficult situations in his life. Drew makes it a point to only focus on what he can control in life and leaves God to take care of the rest.

Drew married his college sweetheart from Purdue University, Brittany, in February of 2003. He and Brittany have three sons and a daughter and live in the Uptown neighborhood of New Orleans. The family still owns a home in San Diego and they often go back in the off-season.

Two of Drew's nicknames include "Breesus" and "Cool Brees", in large part because the New Orleans Saints fans were initially very intrigued by his ability to remain calm under pressure. Drew's league popularity was really shown when he was voted by the fans to be the cover athlete of EA Sports' *Madden NFL 11* video game.

Drew's likability has helped him off the field as well. He has served on the NFL Players Association's Executive Committee since 2008. He has also been featured in many different commercials and advertisements, including becoming the national spokesperson for AdvoCare International.

Chapter 5:

Philanthropic/Charitable Acts

Among casual fans, Drew is almost as well known for his charitable works off the field as he is for his astronomical statistics on the field. His 2010 Sportsman of the Year Award by *Sports Illustrated* was given for both his outstanding play in the postseason but also for his incredible work in the rebuilding of the communities in New Orleans.

During the year 2003, Drew and Brittany worked to create the Brees Dream Foundation. The foundation's mission is to help cancer patients and fund research to help with the disease. Brittany's aunt passed away from cancer and it greatly affected her family. The Brees Dream Foundation has been a great help in the rebuilding of New Orleans after Hurricane Katrina. It currently still funds and facilitates a multitude of programs in the San Diego, California and West Lafayette, Indiana areas, where Drew and Brittany have roots. The foundation has already contributed close to $6 million in donations to help further their mission statement.

In 2007, Drew and Brittany announced a big partnership with the international children's charity, "Operation Kids". The charity's goal is to re-develop facilities for the under-privileged youth in the New Orleans area. These facilities include parks, playgrounds, after-school programs, and child care facilities. In the years since Drew has partnered with Operation Kids, there has been a great impact felt in the community of New Orleans.

Among other notable activities that Drew is involved in, includes a promotional deal with Chili's to help raise money for charity, as well as being the co-chair of the *President's Council on Fitness, Sports and Nutrition*. Drew was personally appointed by President Barack Obama to hold the position of co-chair. Additionally, Drew made an appearance in an anti-bullying video that was well-distributed in late 2010.

Chapter 6:

Legacy, Potential & Inspiration

Drew has become a legend in Louisiana because of the compassion that he showed when the city needed it the most. Furthermore, his charisma and fire is shown on the football field and he is well-known for his ability to pump up his teammates before big games.

Because Drew's era is filled with quarterbacks that fill up the stat sheet, he is often over-looked when it comes to the discussion of the best quarterbacks in the game. Players like Peyton Manning, Aaron Rodgers, and Tom Brady are usually mentioned before Drew and the fact that he plays for a small market team certainly doesn't provide the public as many opportunities to watch him on Sundays. Nevertheless, if you take a look at the record books, it becomes obvious that Drew is one of the best to ever play the position.

He has overcome the perceived limitations that were put on him by scouts when he initially entered the league. His lack of arm strength is no longer part of the discussion and his agile feet and ability to get the ball out quickly has allowed him to work around his height limitation. Whether he is able to lead the Saints to another Super Bowl victory is yet to be seen, but what is certain is that Drew has created a legacy that will be remembered for generations to come. Already known as the greatest New Orleans Saint to ever lace them up, he has become representative with the blue-collar culture of the city of New Orleans.

The family's home inside the city of New Orleans has also made him much more likable to the fans. Unlike many wealthy residents, he keeps in contact with the people in the city proper and does not give off the "untouchable" vibe. Because of this, the city has embraced him as someone who is authentic in his words and actions.

Maybe Drew's best quality is his ability to stand for issues that he believes in. His polarizing personality shines through in situations where controversy is in the air. Whether he is addressing the rules on the field, the issues in a community, or events like "Bountygate", Drew is able to respond with answers that will make you question your own pre-conceived notions.

Chapter 7:

Notable Statistics & Career Milestones

Here is a list of accomplishments that Drew has achieved in his career so far:

College:

- Big Ten Offensive Player of the Year (2000)

- Big Ten MVP (2000)

- Outback Bowl MVP (1999)

- Alamo Bowl MVP (1998)

National Football League:

- AP NFL Comeback Player of the Year (2004)

- NFL Offensive Player of the Year (2008, 2011)

- Super Bowl XLIV MVP (2009)

Conclusion

I hope this book was able to help you gain inspiration from the story of Drew Brees, one of the best players currently playing in the National Football League. At the same time, he is one of the nicest guys outside the gridiron, willing to help out teammates and give back to fans. Last but not least, he's remarkable for remaining simple and firm with his principles in spite of his immense popularity.

The rise and fall of a star is often the cause for much wonder, but most stars have an expiration date. In football, once a star player reaches his mid- to late-thirties, it is often time to contemplate retirement. What will be left in people's minds about that fading star? In Drew's case, people will remember how he led his team in their journey towards a Super Bowl. He will be remembered as the guy who plucked his team from obscurity, helped them build their image, and honed his own image along the way.

Drew has also inspired so many people because he is the star who never failed to look back, who paid his dues forward by helping thousands of less-fortunate youth find their inner light through sports and education. And another thing that stands out in Drew's history is the fact that he never forgot where he came from. As soon as he had the capacity to give back, he poured what he had straight back to those who needed it, and he continues to do so to this day.

Hopefully you learned some great things about Drew in this book and are able to apply some of the lessons that you've learned to your own life! Good luck in your own journey!

Other Football Stories That Will Inspire You!

Calvin Johnson

http://www.amazon.com/dp/B00HJK0YS2

Tom Brady

http://www.amazon.com/dp/B00HJYQTRS

Aaron Rodgers

http://www.amazon.com/dp/B00HJUEDEI

Colin Kaepernick

http://www.amazon.com/dp/B00IRHHABU

Russell Wilson

http://www.amazon.com/dp/B00HK909C8

Peyton Manning

http://www.amazon.com/dp/B00HJUYTCY

Inspirational Basketball Stories!

Stephen Curry

http://www.amazon.com/dp/B00HH9QU1A

Derrick Rose

http://www.amazon.com/dp/B00HH1BE82

Blake Griffin

http://www.amazon.com/dp/B00INNVVIG

Carmelo Anthony

http://www.amazon.com/dp/B00HH9L3P8

Chris Paul

http://www.amazon.com/dp/B00HIZXMSW

Paul George

http://www.amazon.com/dp/B00IN3YIVI

Dirk Nowitzki

http://www.amazon.com/dp/B00HRVPD9I

Kevin Durant

http://www.amazon.com/dp/B00HIKDK34

Other Inspirational Stories!

Mike Trout

http://www.amazon.com/dp/B00HKKCNNU

Miguel Cabrera

http://www.amazon.com/dp/B00HKG3G1W

Buster Posey

http://www.amazon.com/dp/B00KP11V9S

Lou Gehrig

http://www.amazon.com/dp/B00KOZMONW

Babe Ruth

http://www.amazon.com/dp/B00IS2YB48

Floyd Mayweather

http://www.amazon.com/dp/B00HLEX5O6

Anderson Silva

http://www.amazon.com/dp/B00HLBOVVU